THE ODONTIAD
& OTHER POEMS

THE ODONTIAD & OTHER POEMS

The Odontiad & Other Poems

Aaman Lamba

The Odontiad & Other Poems

Copyright © 2020 Aaman Lamba

All rights reserved. No part of this publication may be reproduced, stored in a retrieval system, or transmitted in any form or by any means, electronic, mechanical, photocopying, recording, or otherwise, without written permission of the author and publisher

Published by Aaman Lamba, United States of America

Cover Art by Deepti Lamba

Cover Design by Joseph Lenoir

Audio Book Narration by Miguel Conner

ISBN: 978-1-7345171-3-2

DEDICATION

My family, my dentist, and the taste of memory

Poems

INTRODUCTION	11
Janus	13
Dance!	14
On Boredom	15
Art	17
Surrealist Manifesto #24	18
The Murder	20
Birthday Wishes	21
The Mission	22
Only the Lonely	23
Time of Flight	24
On Writing Poetry	25
Open Hands	27
Moving Pictures	28
Racism is Easy?	30
Silent Mountain	31
To Miss ***	32
The Way of Desire & Memory	34
Colors of Day	36

Happiness Remembered	37
Raw War	39
THE ODONTIAD	41
Sonnet I	43
Sonnet II	44
Sonnet III	45
Sonnet IV	46
Sonnet V	47
Sonnet VI	48
Sonnet VII	49
Sonnet VIII	50
Sonnet IX	51
Sonnet X	52
Sonnet XI	53
Sonnet XII	54
Sonnet XIII	55
Sonnet XIV	56
Sonnet XV	57
Sonnet XVI	58
Sonnet XVII	59
Sonnet XVIII	60
Sonnet XIX	61
Sonnet XX	62

Sonnet XXI	63
Sonnet XXII	64
Sonnet XXIII	65
Sonnet XXIV	66
Sonnet XXV	67
Sonnet XXVI	68
Sonnet XXVII	69
Sonnet XXVIII	70
Sonnet XXIX	71
Sonnet XXX	72
Sonnet XXXI	73
Sonnet XXXII	74
THE POET	77
THE ARTIST	77
THE NARRATOR	77

THE ODONTIAD & OTHER POEMS

INTRODUCTION

I have been writing since I can remember. I've held myself back because if I didn't, I would do nothing else. The words flow, the images flash, the memories crystallize, and time moves on.

When I was in college, I wrote a lot of poetry, often to express my sense of alienation or the feeling that there was more to life than the everyday occurrences which seemed to matter little the next morning. A professor told me I should stick to prose, and my pride hurt, I listened to him and stopped putting pen to verse.

Time, loss, a few preserved poetic images, and freedom from expectations helped me get past the walls I had constructed around this form of the written word as an art form. The Odontiad is a 32-sonnet sequence, initially about the quotidian concept of tooth decay, which expanded to express the nature of decay and collapse in general, and then become a lens through which I could communicate these unusual 'shut-in times'.

The Odontiad and these other poems are now complete and presented for your perusal.

The audio narration by Miguel Conner brings the poems to life.

The cover art by my dear wife, Deepti Lamba, an accomplished artist, is a compelling image which expresses the nature of decay and The Odontiad so well.

THE ODONTIAD & OTHER POEMS

Janus

Falling flowers smoothen the path,
Hiding the thorns which once them attended.
As the petals bereft create the fruit,
So the caterpillar spins its own wombgrave.
> The seconds tick away life, death, and time,
> Marking passages which arrivals leavings are.
> The light of exploding stars,
> Show destruction and illumine lonely abysses.

Leaves die, saving trees from winter's weight,
When they return, no sign of change.
The falling waters wash away arid dirt,
The rock erodes on which sand once was.
> Children grow up, leaving behind their nature,
> Yet adult hearts are one with minds of babes.
> Freedom for the people brings wars,
> Rulers sue for peace, yet only exchange slaves.

The gods playfully their cosmic dice throw,
Planets colliding cause no change in the flow.
The servants of Hell caprice about no less,
Victory's loss 'gainst Good ends not game for Bad.
> The electrons shift and change within you,
> From boundless waves to rigid shapes move .
> This in them doubt creates,
> So it is with their cosmic brethren.

Flashing lightning illuminates natural desire,
Both real and lost in illusion are they all.
The same we see in the one which is main,
Dual Nature of Man is known withal.

Dance!

Dance! With the atomic electrons
as they move on their obeisant orbits,
Each one differently waltzes on,
Yet the same in its circle sits.

Dance! With the laughing fairies
as their sylvan music plays on.
Come swing with the falling berries
and joyfully sing the forest song.

Dance with the planets whirling
As the cosmic rhythm is ascending,
Making poets write happy sonnets
The life of each incarnate unending!

On Boredom

One sits, twiddling one's thumbs
Watching wheeling birds in skies
While all around lie crumbs
And yet in dreams one flies.
One must return
To the humdrum world of men,
Leaving behind the flying tern
Lifting again the useless pen.

> Workers in factories move levers
> Clerks in offices open files
> Each in drifting thought considers
> How to tread the hollow miles
> Human 'progress' suffers
> Unending producing unwanted things
> Who will pay for these errors?
> After all these are human failings.

Man makes efficient machines
Computers begin to compete and run
He wants to recreate his teens
And relive childhood's fun.
His every action usual routine
Each day's work being common.
Could this be an indicator of being?
Fear of the unknown or Mammon?

I sprawl at my cold desk
My thoughts variant with my work
Drawing figures grotesque
Trying to clear the sucking murk,
How do I explain the sorrow
That comes on me when I do the grind?
Shall I leave this deep furrow?
If I do, what hill will I find?

Art

Dear art will not depart
Never will it leave even
If sorrow cuts a part of the heart
And does pass all the passion

    Rex cannot express the same
    Stronger commands than can
    The eyeless images of art's game
    Which gives meaning to man.

All true art spontaneous spouts
From hidden knowledge gowned
In words, thus drowns not in mouths
But comes down to be crowned.

    Hidden motifs within words do sit
    Wonders forgotten in the attic
    Interpretations blend and fit
    Meanings between lines as if in a web stick

Poetry is an untenured property
Now one owner's, now another's
Willing to die to serve this deity
More can none do for mothers

Surrealist Manifesto #24

I heard the mating call
In the lawn outside the hall
'Twas the flat-footed sheep
It's mournful dirge a weep
The captain opened his door
'Ahoy!' he called in a scream
Being disturbed from his dream
When he did hear the foghorn roar
'Bricks ahead!' was the replying wail
These words made him turn pale
'Full steam in my head, my dear!'
He urged them on without fear
'What! Up goes the lid!' cried Watt
'If this were a train, it would be a lot!'
Bogies pulling the engine on the track
They all go clickety-clack
Seeing them, into the field I ran
Without any clue or a plan
'It's elementary, my dear Son,
That the woman is well-done.'
Said Holmes raising the flame
As William took his aim
At the addled egg on his son's head,
Who was meditating on Monroe's bed
While Marilyn was out with John
Seeing good old' Dallas town
Then bang went a gun and out came Lee,

Who swore loyalty and pled amnesty,
Poor Picasso played with poodles
Daft Dali drew dizzy doodles
And caroling Alice flew in a Pan
To Never Never Land with slim Stan
While Hardy dated poor Chaplin
They had a lot of Scotch and gin
'Beam us aboard!' said Kirk
'From the last frontier I won't shirk'
I saw him open the last door
Behind which lay Eve's bastion of yore
Alas! Alack! I heard the toll
Not of tax, but of the bellman's call
The ringer was only Hemingway
And the gong was a Speare o' yesterday
My last sight was the gong's shake
But I saw no more – I was awake
Shaking my head, I turned away
Flapping my tail, swimming in the bay.

The Murder

Death-toned, his face glimmers
The dark disappears in his lamp light
Beside him, blood pools and the body
Dead an hour, the flies arrive soon.
    He looks around, lost in the bushes
    The man lies, motionless and silent
A mile past, he trembles, looks back
Thoughts shift, in time and place
She was beautiful, in an urban way
The man was sitting, hand on hers
He watched, seeing their comfort
Rose and came closer, inhaling her scent
    A stumble, a nudged glass, wetness
        Apologies, the man must leave to dry himself
    He sits, tells her to leave now
    The knife appears, she pales and fades away
The quarry returns, an anger at being left alone
A rushed departure, perhaps to hold her back
Darkness outside the door, the knife sucks in
Then pulling the body to the bushes, later it hits
    The wallet was emptied, with slim pickings
    The fear comes and goes, he shivers
The commission done, but the tension remains
It takes a long time, then he leaves.

Birthday Wishes

The wheel of time and space eternal
Once more turn towards your natal day
What you are moves towards renewal
But what is perfect will forever stay

Live tomorrow in today, let the past be,
Remember happiness, learn from sorrow
Move on, let the meek follow
You will be the pearl of their memories

Time does not stop, let it flow
Everything will happen for good
Your life will show this for all
What should happen would

Thus you will come to know on this happy day
Eternal timeless joy, unsuppressed play.

The Mission

Lying down asleep in sanity
Glowing light shining through
Opening doors of normality
Marking shadowed corridors with life anew
Escaping the labyrinth brings you back around
Revelations are hard to find
Daily labor, from birth to ground
The only reality is the life of the mind
The unheard music is as strong as light
Making more than men of you
Ever striving to set the path right
Bringing order to this mad brew
Like leaves on which falls dew
Let me the way beyond see
Give me direction and a distant view
So I may from mission not flee.

Only the Lonely

Cheek against cheek
in the sweaty heat.
So good we are together,
the way I was.
The curse of the solitary man,
to live with sand in the mouth,
not to understand why,
to cry without tears
for lives unlived save in wasted years.
Petal-butterflies wither
without taking wing.
Regret is total.

Time of Flight

I walk through empty corridors
Searching for I know not what
I see life's closing doors
Leavings and turnings of a sort

    Friends I have and have had
    Flowers I have blossomed in hearts
    Then what is there in me so bad?
    Why do I feel hollow and apart?

I can see before me
Rosy dawns and bright days
Darkness and flashes I flee
Rising into skies and sun's rays

    Hearts crushed by sorrow's burden
    Acceptance only a dream's ecstasy
    Difference a crime in the world of men
    Non-conformity among outsiders a reality

On Writing Poetry

Can the reader ever have thought
Of the long hard battles fought
While trying to confirm to prosody
So as not to make a clumsy parody?
Looking for rimes for dreams and ecstasy
Descending into realms of fantasy
The long hours spent on anthologies
Tragedies forcibly termed into comedies
Words formed or read in tones dulcet
So as to fitfully end a couplet
Syllables that should be Alexandrine
Or perhaps sometimes Florentine
Metric feet that follow the iamb
Like shepherds leading the lamb
Or variations on the pentameter
Trochaic for iamb as in commuter.
Pages torn being so common,
Art sold in pursuit of Mammon.
It is in good/bad poetry
That alliteration appears abundantly,
Sometimes swept in so subtly.
Can men comment on time spent
Whence doth commence consonance?
Most verse seen as retort
By a poet trying to contort
Words for their meanings,
Extracting unwanted gleanings.

Critics replying with scansion
If harmed or given condemnation
Rarely, if any, hope of resurrection.
Empty pages filled with hurt
Clearing away from life dirt
Brought there by words curt
All poetry must be seen
As part-glimpses thru' a screen
Behind which lie glittering
Fire-thoughts flittering
Dreams brought down by pen
Into the cold world of men
Poets trying to hopefully reveal
The Reality behind the seal
Hoping and praying in the end
That mankind will commend.

Open Hands

I hold out to you my hands
Take them, I need the rest
Together, we shall go to happy lands
All that toil – have I passed the test?
    Can you see the wounds, the scars?
    Memories of battles lost and won
    They are gained in reaching for the stars
    One is burned flying close to the sun.
Are they withered? Are they bent?
Does blood flow from the holes?
In work and in life they were rent
Daily changing clothes, wearing new roles.
    These are the hands of a poet, a soldier
    Facing battles, saving others' burdens
    Now that I can see you coming so near
    Past life does appear through fading lens
My hands I clasp over my weak heart
Madness ate my soul, left my mind
Hot memories, cold ones form a part
In me joy, sadness, regret I find
    With many on the road I did meet
    Their notes added subtle essences to my tone
    Bodies, words, food with them did I eat
    Yet in life I came, and I go all alone.

Moving Pictures

I see you through
Sepia-toned memories
So many faces known
The past is many Me's.
Visited and seen places
Happenings out of context
Triggering chains of life
Some happy, others vexed.
That day I had laughed
Other nights, we played
Frozen, captured in time
Living on after I'm dead.

The faces hide tales
Anger, hope, sorrow, all
Reaching into the past
Your face I touch, I call
Companions, moral reversals
Old friends, not easy enemies
These bring realization now
I see what will be, was
No changes can time allow
Effect controls the cause.
But, given another plunge,
Walk the path once again
Save one, I wouldn't change

Once done, you love the pain.
All I want is to try and say,
Somehow show others the way,
Live the rest in a cloud,
And do tomorrow after today.
So that in futures past,
I might say 'twas done,
And done well in life.
Lived with sadness, fun,
Gave much, savored joy.
Pictures blur, senses hum,
We must breathe and die.

Racism is Easy?

Black man in
White boy's room
Will die soon,
Says master Sam.
If you look straight,
And whisper rebellion
You are a mad man,
Black lions jump higher,
Says the panther,
But feel the lash,
That takes our power
From the People
To the people,
Now is the hour!
The time has come!
Death to the other!
I love my brother!

Silent Mountain

The silent mountains call me.
I look to them, I cry.
Trapped as I am by the cold city,
Surrounded by steel cliffs,
Hemmed in by walls of glass.
The people, the crevasses from up high,
Flashes of green, gone too soon,
As pebbles on a hillside,
Pilgrims searching for the way,
Finding what they don't seek.
They move, shift, fall, rise 'gain,
Breathing, suffering, feeling pain.
Stone-like, eroding away,
Like death up high, for many who climb,
The universal city exacts a price
From all who assail the peaks
Of the silent towers around.
Death comes quickly, or not,
Their creations, hopes, dreams die,
Like edelweiss by the mountainside.
Some reach glory of summits uncrowned
And look beyond to the prize.
Victory is sweet, yet easily taken
By climbers coming up the trail.
The road uneven, rest a prize,
We must climb or die,
Because it is what a mountain is for.

To Miss ✱✱✱

Translated by me from French Manuscripts, an introduction to the fairy tale Griselidis, author unknown

By offering you, young & wise beauty,
This model of patience,
I do not flatter myself
Let it be imitated by you on every front
It would be too much, in truth,
But Paris, where men are polite
And the fairer sex is born to please,
Find their happiness accomplished
It is filled everywhere
With examples of vice,
That one cannot in any case
Keep or avoid
Having too much poison
A lady so patient
As the one I describe here
Would be astonishing anywhere,
But is a real prodigy in Paris,
Women are sovereign there,
Everything is settled by their wishes.
Finally, it is a happy environment
Which is inhabited only by queens.

So, I see that, anyway,
Griselidis will be little appreciated there,
And she will laugh at this,
And its antiquated lessons.
It is not that patience
Is merely a virtue of the ladies of Paris,
But by long use, they have the skill
To have it exercised by their own husbands.

The Way of Desire & Memory

Pages torn out of history
Tell tales which come again
For what is past is in the mind
The keeper of future is memory

    The shell which o'er me survives
    Dies with the gun, but it hides
    That which cannot be held
    By men such as walk the world.

To learn the large reality,
First give up the small failings
Brought about by deeds past
Of men gone and not forgotten.

    Then see the flower that is the bud
    The fruit in time to come
    The time that is already past in the past,
    For the future is but a slave to the old.

Now look around your life, your hollow case,
See the world within a pea, the pea to be
Life within, desire is the seed
Pleasure is power, even in denial

Let the seed be a tree,
Then look for the circle without end.
The beginning is the goal of all quests
We are born when we die.

Turn the world inside out its skin
Flying through stars till you return
Holding a tear of Eros,
The pearl of great price,
Hiding it from the world that cannot see.

No more will I need say when you are done,
The truth you will see and smile, laugh,
For what you searched for was in the heart,
Come now and enjoy the living feast.

Colors of Day

Of many shapes and kinds is beauty
Mountains high and seas a-wavy
Eagles soaring above horses sinewy
Cascading waters making riverine fairies
Childhood memories, joy of eternal amity
Hearts coming to oneness, mates in mirth
Past enemies, now friendship does birth
Actions passionate, uncaring for worth.

There are tones and sorts of darkness,
Nights' depths around gloom's mess
Blindness of ignorance, pangs of loneliness
Poverty's dismal colors, wealth's servitude
The greatest hearts broken by life crude
Ebony faces seen in nights-o'-the new moon
Evil's minions dancing blankly to the devil's tune
Also eclipsed glories, a great life's ruin.

Varied are the hues and shades of life
Fair as sunlight or dark as strife
For it joins like glue and cuts like a knife
Burns like fire and leaves like a rainbow
Angry red days, blue moods at dusk
Soft green walks in woods, the anguish of should've
Birth is desire, there's a lot to fill in life's husk
The color that joins all is love.

Happiness Remembered

Pictures in frames, notes in words
Birds with broken wings
Eyes saying unspoken things
Evanescent breaths in the cold air blurred
All these were yours and mine.
Our camaraderie and dreams
In that proud, desperate time,
Held us like firm beams,
The world our oyster was
We were fishing in stormy seas,
Our life needed not a cause,
For it did us both please.

Serving others' appetites,
Building their hopes
Roles played for the lights
Love made us play games.
To the wet streets we did belong,
Looking for a break in life,
Always singing a love song,
Yet keeping ready our sheath knife.

Looking through misty years
Wet snows, cold rains,
Our laughter, our tears,
We had no need to restrain.
A breath, the forever length of time does explain

All we endured and went through
All the struggles and labor
I understand now in memory's view
What kept us going was ardor,
And for this I do thank you.

Raw War

We live in our hollow shells,
Hoping for salvation.
Trying to escape private hells,
Half-believing in resurrection.

    We send others' children
    To fight unseen enemies.
    Giving each one a Bren,
    Forgiving them their felonies.

We beat spades into knives,
Thrusting missiles we send,
Granting death to innocent lives,
How shall we amend?

    How shall the Gods we face?
    What judgements will we meet?
    Will they condemn the human race?
    Will history end in defeat?

THE ODONTIAD & OTHER POEMS

THE ODONTIAD

THE ODONTIAD & OTHER POEMS

Sonnet I

Pearlies, intimate censors of inner
Wonders - that which they deny
Never ventures on the fantastic voyage
Of Organon's dominions; systems
That propagate life, build walls
And epidural towers; man's body.
> Mastication of organoids, then process
> Causing micturition; proto-human creation
> Of organa; fertilization, growth,
> The fruit ripens, encounters the white warriors
> A spiraling procession that never ends
> Save when arrives a stronger, seductive evil.
> Sugary greed, insidious disease, decay of age
> Gaps in the pearly gates, then emptiness.

Sonnet II

Candidly contemplate commercial corporate clarity
Brought about, without doubt, by gamut of cosmetics
Turning yellowed tusks into consumer-friendly whites
To attract, not orthodontal purity, but Mammon's Vesta
Hygienically tending to sinister left and dexterous right
Submissive slave, addictive Hierophant to a blind God.
    All the same, we take our chances to gain
    What we can achieve, not through servile labor,
    Rather, by alleys & yards of Morality's Temple
    The succor of diabetic, orgasmic, sweet path,
Followed by a low, not post-coital, but pre-dental.
A path from common quietude to white heaven.
Valhallic respite, then doom, both economic
And aged empty gums infantile.

Sonnet III

First, there was not even the void,
Nay, semiotic fluid, giving meaning, forming, shaping,
From oneness to multiplicity, creating
Homuncular-like, then hardness, bone white
Stoic forms, archetypal incisors, destroyers,
Indiscriminate occlusion leading to the trembling
Then betrayal, loss, once again the void.

The birth of rocks is accompanied by fire,
Bursting forth and breaking through, but burning out,
As do these ghastly barriers, liberating one from labors
chameleonic, another step towards entropic Nirvana,
Leaving its lacerations on the past.

Who can say if this is a loss or a gain, leaving a pain?
Perhaps a glimmer of other agonies, felt in juvenilia?

Sonnet IV

- Selected for the Virginia Bards Poetry Anthology 2020

Nothing ever came from nothing, nothing could
Yet when I feel the serrated gaps, I wish it would.
My life a constant pain, only memories sweet,
Seeing so many others smiling in the street.
>As I lie shivering 'neath this tarp,
>The windy city chills my heart.
>Slowly reaching for a coin,
>In this bitter and cruel Tenderloin.

Can you satisfy your greed
With the tremors of my need?
There's nothing wrong with loving
And craving the needle's sting.
We take what we can, we want, we need,
And everything is guaranteed.

Sonnet V

The solitary times are not for me.
Rather, my sanctuary is in the world,
The brilliant, glistening, enameled age.
I would burnish the stains and fill in the gaps,
Make you whole and intact.
Restore the memory and the joy,
Until we were all lustrous and radiant.
I know this is a dream unbound.
You might want the grand hotel,
Hiding in the shadows of your cave,
Curling your scorpion tail,
Sealing your curmudgeonly shell,
Letting the bell ring,
Until winter covered spring.

Sonnet VI

The fear of the reaper holds me fast
I clutch the arms of this glistening chair
It's familiar white seat
The pneumatic engine throbbing beside
I tremble as the drill hums
The mask looms before me
His gloved hands grasp my face,
Turning me to him
He molds me like clay
And with a smile captures my heart
Time passes swiftly
Until I must return
My need so strong
And the will so weak.

Sonnet VII

This gun for hire, a hitman of pleasure,
I am the heavy hitter of the pack.
Thrusting, piercing, grinding,
We dirty dozen are the main crew,
Holding the fort, custodians of wisdom.
We listen to your fears and pain,
Clenching, crushing, and hitting the pedal,
Our dreaming is your nightmare.
      There is a darkness at our root
      Which inflamed, makes us rebel
      We pass secret messages in hidden channels
      Fill our moats with rancid poison
      Raise bestial armies of fecund monsters
      Until heavy artillery comes to bring us to heel.

Sonnet VIII

In the year of the rat, when we were shut in,
You and I rediscovered each other
As the old folks saw their boom wane
And iron men stuck to their magnetic fields
Reshaped the world in invisible ways,
While the sky wheel turned over empty streets,
And fallen angels made another trip to earth.
    We were tired of living our solitary lives,
    Barred from the towers and shelters
    Scavenging, feeling serrated holes
    Where our raw tongue slipped through,
    And we hacked our coughs dry
    Using sheets of gold, so soft.
    All those wasted years, so much time.

Sonnet IX

It was early summer when we went down to the cape,
That year, the oleanders had bloomed early
The pink and red flashes as we drove past,
Folks were parking, unloading, sitting on the porch
We felt it would be a good season.
The pampas had been freshly cut; traffic was light.
I craned my neck to see which movies were on
They had a *Star Wars* marathon this weekend
I wished they would do a *Jaws* special, slim chance.
As we turned the curve and passed the inn,
We noticed the parking lot was full
I made a note to call ahead for the evening dinner.
There was a sense of anticipation now,
We deserved a break after all the pain.

Sonnet X

Sometimes, one must let go,
The future is adaptation
To the memories of the past.
Rebellion, refusal, reconciliation
    Don't give up the taste, the feeling,
    This is not the end, it is not terminal
    We've dealt with worse,
    Passive hope steals possibility,
What if tomorrow is not like yesterday?
We deny our magic and the wonder of reality
We are creators, this is our universe
Don't play by the rules of the game,
Radical change is our choice,
And so is resilience.

Sonnet XI

A change in the air, our last flights from the coast,
Summer plans half-made, promises not kept
The black serpent writhes its silent dance
Flowers blossom, wither in the night
Jazz notes in the evening breeze
As our world is born and made.
    Small changes, everything is different
    Valentine's day was cold, the twilight came fast,
    Then we were home for a long while
    The rain came down, it was a brilliant spring
    We had all the time in the world to love
    We loved the world in our time
    There was a grey mist to tomorrow,
    No messages crackled through the ether.

Sonnet XII

We were given the keys
To the kingdom of heaven
By the four chiefs in their quarters.
The princes of the Angels stood guard
Over the wasteland and the joy,
As we relived our anamneses,
and every moment sang a note of creation:
Do this in memory of me
Let the blood flow and be cherished
For its liturgy of remembrance.
The vessel is the door,
The journey is the message,
Strangers are our own company,
As we find our gnosis in understanding.

Sonnet XIII

-for Elise Cowen

The Beat women, those starlight flowers,
Who moved us from under our feet,
And wrote letters through time to past and future
Lovers, who were as far away
As angels might be from their rebel sisters in hells,
Birthing their lovers' demons in their nunneries,
Unable at last to pass the time in the hollow days.
Dead inside and the methedrine would not hold,
Living for others like most women do,
Déshabillé Amazons choking their emotions,
Girl meets boy, love follows,
But it's too late to hide the shame and bury the pride.
Jack, you legend of the new Romantics,
Elise of the open window, no one to say Kaddish for you

Sonnet XIV

There is weeping and gnashing of teeth.
It is the end of the age of power,
And Hermes wipes the slate clean
As he sharpens his stylus of the new eon.
We rebel our will and hold fast to the narrow gate,
The thrones are weakened by borers silent.
Violence will not gentle the savage heart
Until the weakest is at peace with the strong.
  Two ships set out from a safe harbor.
  Storms were set on the path of one,
  Yet the other was last to reach its goal.
  We pray to the end of cruel winds,
  Still waters, for the puissant and the wretched,
  Before we set forth for home again.

Sonnet XV

The gamer lives and dies again
I am the master of my domain
Laughing in my playground,
As I dance to the jester's sound,
Drawing my energy sword of light
On the dark bosses of night,
Or the blades of chaos feared
In my muscled skin seared.
Falling bricks must not hold
Before the windows of time are closed
Cities of memory and art
Civilizations form, grow, fall apart
Princes saddle horses, ride forth
Dangers lie waiting to the North.

Sonnet XVI

If every birth were a fall, the light in the void
Coming into our world, a glimmer of the whole,
We would be more than our fragile selves.
Our breath carrying a song of glory,
Nights under the moon striving for the crown,
Fleeting beauty, balancing strength and mercy.
> The world is our kingdom, our power and glory,
> Moments our currency of worth.
> The texture slipping, sliding away,
> A midwinter dream of endless summer nights,
> Until all we have left are stories untold,
> Memories and regrets of loves foretold.
> The paths taken blur and weave,
> A moment more, before I leave.

Sonnet XVII

My astral temple is a resort on a hill.
It overlooks the sea, and has a path into the forest,
There is a lake with large fishes and tall green trees.
My guardians are tall black forms; when I'm away,
They take the shape of sinuous snakes in the grass,
Sometimes, kingfishers diving in the lake.
There is a cave in the woods, with a living computer,
Which contains all worlds and all memories.
When things are gone, they are not forgotten.
This is my utopia, a counter-spell to the entropy.
The air is sweet, it is mine forever and free,
There are no masks or dungeons unless I so choose.
Caprio and Santa Muerte lounge by the pool,
As I traverse realms with a breath and a whisper.

Sonnet XVIII

Sobek, free me from the bounds of my ego,
Be the dweller on the threshold and trip me up.
When I rise, I fall, I rise again.
My midnight resistance holds the key
Until I come again.
The beat of my secret heart
Is the lightning pulse of creation
In the darkness of the world.
L'aube abime, arrive enfin
Toujours pour vous, c'est mon espoir[1]
I am ensnared in the worlds,
The deepest love is that we let go,
Merge into the ten thousand things,
One becomes two and three evermore.

---

[1] The engulfing dawn arrives finally
Forever yours, I do hope and pray

Sonnet XIX

I saw a coyote at the crossroads, one dark night.
He was the ally I needed during my solitary vigil.
I heard an owl in the distance, not close.

The lamppost casts long shadows in the still air,
The stars glitter like teeth in the boundless ocean.
The hours never leave as the memories breathe,
Anchored in the sands of time.
We go forward, we turn back, we follow our paths,
Carving our runes in the dirt,
Like maverick prophets of a new age
Until the grand design is known.

The pale fire of dawn cleared the gloom,
I had burned another night away, idling the moments,
Closer and closer to the infinite darkness.

Sonnet XX

Two cups of emotion, scooped from the heart,
A wee dram of tears wept on lonely nights.
Moments of laughter, to lighten the load,
Sprinkled with joy, drawn from casks of memories,
Stirred together in companionship that binds
With congealed words left unspoken.
And yet what would you not give
For one more breath, one more whispered word,
A last kiss, a lone sock cast aside in haste,
As love took hold and the world was lost?
The empty mirror, the silent room,
The unwatched episodes, the unread books,
Time enough and more, days without end,
Hold fast until I die.

Sonnet XXI

A glimmer of black, a flicker of white,
It began with a flash, a spark, a quiver,
It will end with the hush of silence, darkness around.
Hope dies, but not the search for the other.
Alone in the night, I call your name, feel your presence,
Your image glimmers, but you're not there.
My restless heart cleans up the shards,
As your scent still lingers in the empty room,
I hold fast to your ephemeral smile.
We'll be together again; I'll kiss you in the summer rain,
Every chord of every song we heard will measure
The first and last moment of our forever time
I will bear the cross with nails of bliss,
Until I am raised by your kiss.

Sonnet XXII

A light shone through you
Neither sun nor star could equal thee
Why then could you not see
Eternal love shining through?
Dark abysses, glowing embers
The closer I got, the deeper I fell
Tracing salt lines through arid seas
Looking into oblivion, hours a-bed
Flashes of joy, momentary splendor
That never held, never died.
I was your willing toy in the forever game
Words aren't held true
Love is blinding and intense,
                    Hold fast, never die.

Sonnet XXIII

Atlantean obsidian walls collapsing on each other
While we searched for safe haven across violent seas
Ball games left for final battles on Andean slopes
Desert sands consuming our rivers of gold
Escaping our cliff dwellings as the stars fell
Cedar walls crushing hopes under Mississippian floods
Moai bereft of offerings while we ate the last seeds
Holding hands while the blades clashed and stung
Silent halls where once knights dined on plates of gold
Damascene legacy crushed under avarice and hate
How many times will we build our hopes?
How many ages must the darkness withhold?
Is there no escape for the prey from the predator?
The slate is cleaned for another creator.

Sonnet XXIV

Anubis' feather or one from an angel's wing,
The withering o' the green,
As leaves fall in the snow,
I soar, I rise, I fall.
My lovers leave in the night,
There is no shelter in the rain for me,
Sipping sake from a warm cup
After an evening tryst.
We are lost in the labyrinth of our lives,
Sleeping Beauty in a forever dream.
Creating worlds, Prozac dulls the pain
The red pill makes you hunger,
The blue lasts longer.
Look closely, but don't go deeper.

Sonnet XXV

We have a long mirror in the upstairs living room,
It has an ornate frame, with curls and grand flourishes.
Anyone who looks at themselves in it feels unsettled.
They ask us if we feel it too, we nod and shrug,
We don't mention the whispers, the glimmer beyond,
It feels a doorway to a palace of possibilities.
We've told each other many tales about its history,
Each adding a layer of myth and wonder.
We keep its true origins hidden within the family,
Even then, we blur the time, place, and names.
It might be a Civil War ancestor's dark ritual enshrined
In the glass and wood, until a young Slave couple
     stepped through and were gone.
Perhaps from Europe, the red flecks a memory of evil,
Or a purchase from a traveler with a glint in his eye.

Sonnet XXVI

The American journey, fed by many rivers
All the world's heritage, the imperfect union,
The wild gods and the shadow paths,
Have led us to this uncertain redoubt.
We hide behind our walls and our masks,
Waiting the unending year out.
Fire, wind, grandstanding, and pain
Until we should dance again.
    The hard trials of this bitter century
    Nurturing the Zoom generation,
    Demanding a reckoning for the past,
    Even as the new world was born,
    Through the resistance of the old
    And the desires of the few.

Sonnet XXVII

Do you remember when the Earth
Was lit up by a ring of satellites
Packed closely together with a beam
Of light from one to the other?
We all looked up in awe that night
As our world became a beacon of delight.
Dawn of a new age, the firmament renewed,
Our hopes were so fresh and full,
All the centuries of toil and struggle,
The labor of steam and patina of rust,
Millenia of pain, pyramids of dust.
We would stride across galaxies,
Raise flags in arenas of gold,
If only our dreams and luck would hold.

Sonnet XXVIII

To love war, to course through history on a pale horse,
Blood on the field, cities of gold left in dust,
My fathers sacked Troy and Ilium, I took Illyricum,
I was sole lord of the Goths.
Magister militum, bellator summus[2]
The greatest feasts the world had ever known,
A thousand cattle and tithes of mead,
A ring from a lady fair that gave me the West,
A castle of skulls and crowns at my feet,
To ride without rest, Mars by my side.
I had the world and forevermore,
Until a Getic flower pricked her thorn
In my side, on the high night of our lives,
I fell, a reed in the marshes.

---

[2] *Gratias ad Andrew Snowdon et Logan Seth Bishop*

Sonnet XXIX

A covey of sparrows lives in the boxwoods
And green holly outside my window.
They twitter and keep me company as I write.
When I step outside for a breath of fresh air,
They scatter with a flourish of noise and wings,
But return soon, searching for food among the trees.
In fall, they look at me as if to ask for seed,
I make sure the feeders are well-stocked.
A pair tries every year to make a nest in the eaves,
Laboring even when the wind blows the twigs away.
I don't think they recognize my step,
But I like to hope they see me as a friend
And a protector of their tribe, from the hawk
Who lies in wait in the pines nearby.

Sonnet XXX

- for Marilyn Manson

Death is a slow process; the plans begin to fray.
Every feverish day beats a slow pace on the drum.
The tempo grows slower, skips a breath,
Until the last stroke and the fury ebbs.
The black planet, the sinking sun, the hidden star.
So much still to do, no shoulder to bear the cross,
The uncapped pen, stiffened brush, fallen petal.
What lies beyond, will the bird have wings?
There will be time enough and more, skies and stone,
The eternal convalescence, the historical moment,
No more fighting, following, or loving, a surfeit of time
An involuntary leisure, the measure of mortality
That is without mourning, the inferno of you,
Burning quickly, through and through.

Sonnet XXXI

- for the Archangel Michael, Conner Habib

Flaming swords flashing, the shining lion Michael
Shows the way, he points through the apocalypse.
Love your enemy, see the spirit in the material world,
A thousand helpers shaping the moment and morrow
On this emerald pearl of great price, above and below.
Our cities will be built up and they will fall.
The ships reach their harbor, the bells toll.
Winter will turn to summer, waves to sand
Until we leave the ways of the world
Into the immanent infinite presence.
Free us from the traps of the enemy,
Release us from our chains of gold and salt.
Guide us to the farther shore,
Be daughter, son, mother, ghost.

Sonnet XXXII

Children of earth, lords of fire, seraphim of air
Seeing our nature and no other,
the alchemy of return cleanses,
We come round again,
until we have stopped stopping.
We are here and there, not aware.
In time, we are out of time,
Wandering, wondering, awakening.

Ten steps on the path, one more,
Searching in the grass, the ox is not seen.
Sitting in the sunlight, the shadow is close.
Games unplayed, the pilgrim goes on,
Crossing an abyss of good and one of evil.
We are the magical ronin of no master.

THE ODONTIAD & OTHER POEMS

THE ODONTIAD & OTHER POEMS

THE POET

Aaman Lamba is a poet, occultist and student of magic, astrology, and philosophy, as well as a computer science professional. His articles have been published in leading newspapers. He was the editor and publisher of an online magazine. He lives in Virginia.

Other books by Aaman include The Complete Illustrated Grand Grimoire from the original French manuscripts and an anthology of selected occult romances from noted French authors. He is currently working on additional translations of texts that deserve greater attention as well as a book on ways of engaging with the world for solitary magicians.

THE ARTIST

Deepti Lamba is an accomplished self-taught artist with her works in private collections and featured in shows. Her art can be found at BlueSigil.com

THE NARRATOR

Miguel Conner is an accomplished podcaster and audio expert, as well as a Gnostic savant. He is the host of Aeon Byte Gnostic Radio, a popular show that takes audiences from ancient mysteries to a modern meaning. He can be contacted at TheGodAboveGod.com for insights and audio narration

www.ingramcontent.com/pod-product-compliance
Lightning Source LLC
Chambersburg PA
CBHW031459040426
42444CB00007B/1146